Original title:
The Christmas Tree's Silent Story

Copyright © 2024 Creative Arts Management OÜ
All rights reserved.

Author: Maya Livingston
ISBN HARDBACK: 978-9916-94-372-4
ISBN PAPERBACK: 978-9916-94-373-1

Hearthside Reflections of the Past

In the corner, a pile of toys,
Remember me? Oh, those raucous boys.
The cat's on the tree, but she's not allowed,
Judging us all, looking oh-so-proud.

Grandma's fruitcake, a holiday slap,
We all take a bite—then hold our nap!
With laughter and love, we gather near,
Each quirky moment brings festive cheer.

Threads of Gold and Silver Gleam

Tinsel hangs low, a shimmering mess,
Cats think it's lunch—now that's anyone's guess!
The ornaments swing like they're in a dance,
Swatting through branches, oh, what a chance!

A star on the top, but it seems a bit wobbly,
Even the lights look a bit too knobbly.
As we sip our cocoa, we can't help but grin,
With all of these antics, let the fun begin!

The Silent Watcher of Wishes

A candle flickers, but what's that I see?
A ghost cat pretending to climb up a tree!
With laughter we gather around its great height,
On a mission to spot all the shimmery light.

Uncle Bob's snoring sounds like a song,
As we tangle in garlands, it won't take long.
Wishes on cards, flung high with a laugh,
Who knew our dreams would take such a path?

Beneath the Blinking Stars

Outside, the snow falls in fragile delight,
But inside, the chaos is quite a sight.
Spilled popcorn strings and a sweet, sticky brew,
A party of mishaps, just us and the crew.

The moon is a witness to our silly spree,
As we toast to the joys of holiday glee.
Laughter erupts, as we dance with a cheer,
Spinning in circles, warmth grows all year.

A Chill of Anticipation in Air

Lights are tangled in a mess,
My dog thinks it's a new game,
He tumbles through the shiny dress,
Now he's the one to blame.

Ornaments hang like low-hanging fruit,
Busy cats eye the shiny spree,
One swipe, it's a holiday hoot,
Now there's chaos beneath the tree.

Pine needles rain like little darts,
As kids race to grab a treat,
They're stealing pinecone art parts,
While giggling in their little fleet.

With every jingle, hopes arise,
For candy canes and gifts galore,
But surprise! A sock is the prize,
What's Christmas without some lore?

Evergreen Dreams Beneath the Stars

Underneath the stars so bright,
A squirrel thinks it's his new home,
He's got his eye on ornaments' light,
Planning mischief with a roam.

Snowflakes dance like disco balls,
The kids are dressed in fuzzy hats,
They trip and giggle down the halls,
Who knew pine could attract such brats?

With cocoa cups, we hold them high,
While marshmallows fight for their place,
One lands perfectly, oh my!
Hot chocolate's the ultimate race.

The night wraps up with songs so loud,
Who knew we'd hit the wrong note?
We're tumbling amidst laughter proud,
With more giggles than we'd ever wrote!

A Tale Weaved in Winter's Embrace

The kitten's found the tinsel bright,
In her paws, it twirls and twirls,
She leaps for joy in pure delight,
As the glittering chaos unfurls.

Baking cookies, flour flies,
Little hands make quite a mess,
They try to measure, what a surprise,
We're left with a sweetened stress!

Each gift unwrapped is a wild spree,
"Oh look, it's socks!" we all agree,
Yet laughter rings with glee so free,
For fun is better than great decree.

The carols echo through the room,
Mixing voices out of tune,
But we're all dreaming through the gloom,
Finding joy beneath the moon.

Branches Holding Memories

In the corner stands a pine,
Holding secrets, oh so fine.
Gossip of the cats who play,
And kids who dance and shout all day.

Underneath, the gifts entice,
Wrapped in paper, oh so nice.
But wait! A nibble here or there,
Seems like snacks are everywhere!

Branches sag with tales so tall,
Of ornaments that bravely fall.
Each little bulb a story told,
Like that time dad went for gold.

And while we laugh, the lights will blink,
Sharing joy—oh, it's the link.
With cookies crumbs and laughter free,
This merry tree holds memory!

Ornaments of Yesteryears

Shiny balls from ages past,
Hanging strong but built to last.
There's a clown with eyes so wide,
And a fake fruit that's got too much pride.

On a branch, a cat will swing,
Chasing baubles in their bling.
A dog's old bone, mistaken gift,
Makes the family smile and lift.

Glittering beads and knitted things,
Talk of relatives and their flings.
Each ornament has learned to tease,
Even uncle's old mustache tease!

With laughter filling up the room,
Old tales dance in vivid bloom.
As lights twinkle in delight,
We all share stories through the night.

A Fir's Gentle Reverie

Oh, a fir with thoughts so sweet,
Dreams of snow beneath its feet.
Chirping birds and whispers low,
Underneath it feels like snow.

It remembers all the fun,
When the kids came out to run.
Sleds and laughter filled the air,
Till mom yelled, 'Get in! You're bare!'

Each year adds a twinkle bright,
With each battle and each fight.
Spilling cocoa on the floor,
Green carpets, oh what a chore!

As candles flicker and tales unfold,
The tree chuckles, feeling bold.
A fir that knows it's quite the star,
In this joyful, silly bazaar.

Shadows of a Winter's Eve

In the night, our shadows dance,
Flitting by with merry prance.
Behind the tree they skip and sway,
Making mischief in a play.

Mom's hot cocoa in our sights,
We sneak sips on secret nights.
Marshmallows adding to the fun,
Mustache of foam when we're done.

Carols sung off-key and loud,
We laugh as dad bursts through the crowd.
With tangled lights and spirits bright,
We'll keep the fun alive tonight.

So here's to stories, laughter tune,
Underneath the glowing moon.
The shadows tell who we all are,
Together, we shine like a star!

Guardians of Yuletide Mystique

In the corner, sparkles shine bright,
Ribbons twist, what a silly sight!
Elves on tiptoes, peeking near,
Whispering secrets just to hear.

A cat dashes by, all in a blur,
Knocking down baubles with a purr.
Jingle bells jangle, oh what a sound,
As mischief and mayhem swirl all around.

A Bough of Hope

A pie baking high on the shelf,
The dog's been eyeing it all by himself.
Tickled by scents of cookies and glee,
He plots his escape, oh what a spree!

With frosting and sprinkles all over the floor,
We grin through the chaos, can't help but adore.
In laughter we gather, with sweets to devour,
Unwrapping the joy, hour by hour.

A Heart of Peace

The lights twinkle brightly, like stars in a race,
Grandpa's snoring adds to the pace.
Mistletoe hanging, but no one to kiss,
Just a reindeer that came to reminisce.

With socks on their hands, they dance very slow,
Spinning around, putting on quite a show.
Laughter erupts, like snowflakes in flight,
Celebrating the season, oh what a night!

Echoes of Laughter in the Fir

A squirrel peeks out from the height of the tree,
Completing the puzzle of who could it be.
With acorns to gather, he jumps to his fate,
But trips on the tinsel and shouts, "not too late!"

Enchanted by whispers and merry old tunes,
The ornaments giggle beneath full moons.
They chime and they jingle in perfect delight,
Spreading the joy through the dark of the night.

The Unfolding Story of December

Wrapped in a blanket, cocoa in hand,
Tales told by the fire, all carefully planned.
The ghost of last Christmas leaps from the box,
With tales of mischief, like sneaking a fox.

As snowflakes descend, they laugh with each glide,
Creating a blanket where giggles can hide.
With hearts full of wonder, we cherish this cheer,
For each year's unfolding is what we hold dear.

Enchanted by the Glow

Lights twinkle bright, like stars in the night,
A squirrel's climbed up, thinking it's quite the sight.
Ornaments wobble, they dance with such glee,
While the cat ponders, 'Is this tree for me?'

A garland of popcorn, oh what a delight,
Until doggies arrive, quick snacks take flight.
Tinsel and glitter spread everywhere fast,
As we laugh and we cheer, this chaos won't last!

Yearning for Yuletide Dreams

Santa's lost sleigh, down the road it did roll,
Reindeer now grazing, out of control.
Bob brings his fruitcake, it's hard as a rock,
We all take a nibble, then promptly just mock.

Mittens and hats, fashion statements so grand,
Even Uncle Joe looks like he's in a band.
With cocoa in hand, we spill on our feet,
The laughter erupts, can't stay in our seat!

Whispers of Evergreen

In the corner, a tree with a secret to tell,
Its branches all swaying like they're under a spell.
Hiding bright treasures, and a sock full of treats,
While Grandma just ponders her warm fuzzy feats.

Chasing the puppy, oh where can he be?
Tangled in strings, wrapped up like a bee.
With laughter we spill, as we tidy the room,
Such joy in the chaos, oh how it'll bloom!

Secrets Wreathed in Pine

Under the boughs, where lost secrets lie,
The elf in the corner thinks he can fly.
A mishap with tinsel, and a grin on his face,
Turns glittery mayhem into a wild race!

Ornaments giggle, "Oh don't let us drop!"
While the kids run around, laughing, they hop.
A whisper of pine, a chuckle so light,
As we cozy together, all's merry and bright.

Beneath the Orbs of Color

Underneath the twinkling lights,
A cat embarks on silly flights.
With tinsel draped around his neck,
He struts like he's the holiday tech.

Mice hang out like party-goers,
They laugh at him, the real decor.
While he swats at shiny things,
Dreaming big of flying wings.

The ornaments swing with a joyful cling,
Our furry friend, he starts to sing.
The floor gets crowded, laughter's keen,
Who knew joy dwells in a Christmas scene?

Luminescence in Stillness

In the quiet of the glowing night,
A squirrel comes to join the bite.
He steals a bulb, oh what a sight,
Has he gone nuts or is he just bright?

The star atop begins to wobble,
As he munches, hear the squabble.
The tree shakes like it's in a dance,
Underneath, nuts roll in a prance.

Little kids in jammies creep,
Their giggles sound like a secret sweep.
Adventurous moments, full of cheer,
With each little jingle, the fun draws near.

Enchanted by Nature's Whimsy

Beneath the branches, a raccoon peeks,
His masked face grins; he's full of tricks.
With jelly beans stuck to his paws,
He searches for treasure without a pause.

The pine scent wraps around his nose,
As he jingles tiny silver bows.
With each step, he leaves behind ash,
His party vibe is quite the splash.

Birds take turns upon the boughs,
Chirping tunes like they're in a house.
While critters gather, the chatter flows,
In this wild show, anything goes.

A Sprig of Hope in Each Adorn

A mouse made camp in a velvet shoe,
Planning a feast for the whole crew.
With crumbs he gathered, a tiny feast,
He laughs at the cat, a furry beast.

Candles flicker with a nervous dance,
While he spins tales in the moonlight's glance.
Spaghetti strands hang like a surprise,
The twinkling lights make magic arise.

With giggles shared, they form a band,
The critters play, a merry hand.
Each ornament hums a silly tune,
This party's full of joy, a festive boon.

Reflection in the Gleam

In twinkling lights, a squirrel hides,
In search of nuts, he giggles and glides.
Round bulbs that shine, he gives a start,
"I'm just a tree with a beating heart!"

A star on top, it wobbles and sways,
While ornaments laugh in their shiny arrays.
The garland's laughing, it's starting to fray,
"Oh, what a mess! It's a holiday ballet!"

Frost-Kissed Whispers

Snowflakes dance on branches up high,
As frosty critters play peek-a-boo, oh my!
"Excuse me, dear elf, could you move along?"
"To this cozy spot, you don't quite belong!"

The lights all flicker, a disco of glee,
As pine cones conspire on what they can see.
"Just let me down, I need to unwind,
These branches are tighter than I'd ever find!"

Shimmering Echoes of Joy

Presents piled high, a mountain of cheer,
A puppy's found toys, he's loaded with gear.
"Oh, what's this one? Can I have a peek?"
"Just a soft squeaker, but so unique!"

Tinsel goes flying, like a cat on the run,
"Did you see my antics? I think it was fun!"
While shadows are dancing, a sprightly parade,
More than a tree, it's a joy parade!

Tales Beneath the Boughs

Under the boughs, a mouse spins a yarn,
Of carols sung loud, and candy that's charmed.
"Did you hear the one about the mistletoe?
It tried to kiss me; oh, what a show!"

A bear with a scarf, he snoozes away,
While giggling lights throw a bright cabaret.
"Shh, don't wake him—let dreams thrive and grow,
For this whimsical night has much more to show!"

Ornaments of Forgotten Dreams

On branches high, they sway and spin,
Forgotten wishes sealed within.
A bulb that once lit up the night,
Now's stuck in glitter, what a sight!

The garland fights with tangled glee,
Its edges whisper, 'set me free!'
A Santa's hat with a droopy ear,
Hides secrets, smiles, and a bit of cheer.

I swear that elf is stealing looks,
His grin more mischievous than books.
As tinsel weaves a tale so bright,
One can't help but chuckle at the sight!

A star that's crooked, lost at sea,
For holiday selectivity.
Yet in this mess, joy is found,
In every laugh, love does abound.

The Language of Twinkling Stars

Above the tree, they blink and glow,
Conspiring tales only they know.
Each flicker hints of quirky cheer,
As jingling bells draw laughter near.

They whisper secrets to the night,
While squirrels dream of their delight.
A comet zips, 'oh what a mess!'
Raining sparkles, they truly bless!

One star claims it's the brightest here,
While others jest, 'we'll outshine fear.'
A dance of lights, a cosmic spree,
Making wishes, wild as can be!

So gather 'round, enjoy the charade,
With every twinkle, joy is made.
Our chortles echo in spaced expanse,
Beneath this twilight, we laugh and dance.

Grace in the Glisten

Glistening ornaments made of glass,
Reflecting giggles as they pass.
A reindeer stuck in a shiny bow,
Is trying hard to steal the show!

With every shimmer, a chuckle flows,
A candy cane that bends and glows.
It tells of sweets, both bright and bold,
In agents of cheer, we're always sold!

A twinkling light, dancing in glee,
Encourages even the shyest tree.
With whispers soft, and jokes so light,
We gather close for sheer delight!

So here's to moments wrapped in grace,
With laughter lighting up the space.
Each shining facet, a story we create,
In this joyous time, we celebrate!

Beneath the Glittering Canopy

Underneath a canopy of cheer,
A chubby elf lingers near.
With belly laughs and twinkling eyes,
He hides the truth behind the lies.

Each ornament has a tale to tell,
Of holiday parties and awkward spells.
An angel winks, 'I've seen it all!'
While tinsel giggles, having a ball!

The little drummer in a silly hat,
Plays off-beat, like a shaggy cat.
As snowflakes drift and start to play,
In this whimsical dance, they sway!

So come and join the festive spree,
Beneath the laughter of this tree.
With hearts aglow and spirits high,
We'll twist and twirl until we fly!

Silent Conversations in the Snow

In the stillness, whispers grow,
Pine needles giggle, don't you know?
Frosty branches sway with glee,
Sharing secrets, just like me.

Snowflakes tumble with a wink,
Caught in laughter, what do they think?
Nearby squirrels hold their breath,
While snowmen plot a chilly death.

A snowball flies, a playful throw,
While giggling twinkles start to glow.
Beneath the lights, a dance begins,
With winter's cheer, there's no room for sins.

So gather 'round with mirth and cheer,
As nature's jests draw us near.
In this stillness, laughter's key,
Amongst the branches, wild and free.

The Yearnings of a Timeless Trio

Three wise men trudge through the night,
Bickering softly, but it's all right.
One's got gold and one's got myrrh,
While the other offers a cinnamon spur.

Their feet are sore on this frosty quest,
Each grumbling softly, doing their best.
"Next time, let's ride," the youngest states,
But they just laugh, leaving behind their plates.

They find a tree with a star on top,
And all their woes begin to drop.
With gifts a-plenty and joy to share,
They forget their troubles, in this festive air.

So here's to laughter, amidst the plight,
And friendship warming the winter's night.
Three souls united in a whimsical spree,
This timeless trio is wild and free.

Beauty Wrapped in Pine's Embrace

A forest whispers, quiet delight,
With ornaments glimmering, a dazzling sight.
The critters peek, it's quite a show,
As the wise old owl says, "Let's go slow."

Bows tied tightly, with colors so bright,
But one little squirrel, what a fright!
He trips on tinsel, takes a great fall,
Yet stands up proudly, claims it's his ball.

The laughter echoes through the green,
While glitter flies, a jolly scene.
Wrapped up in joy, the candles gleam,
In nature's brilliance, we all can dream.

So dance we shall, beneath the boughs,
With all our cocoa and happy vows.
In this embrace, magic is real,
The beauty of laughter is the best deal.

The Unbroken Circle of Light and Love

Around the tree, we take a seat,
With cookies, cocoa, and laughter sweet.
Grandpa struggles to turn on the lights,
While Grandma cackles and playfully bites.

A garland stranded, stuck in the twist,
Makes for a perfect comedic tryst.
"Who put this here?" someone exclaims,
As the dog jumps in, joining the games.

The kids giggle, and the cat's on alert,
Seeking out mischief and some warm flirt.
A romping chaos, a festive delight,
As love wraps 'round, making things right.

So raise a toast to our merry crew,
Filled with joy, and laughter too.
In this circle, we shine so bright,
Together we beam, our love a light.

Reflections Beneath the Glitter

Underneath the shiny baubles,
A cat is plotting grand escapes.
Each time it leaps, I grab my camera,
But all I capture are the scrapes.

Tinsel hangs like tangled thoughts,
The ornaments wear goofy grins.
Santa's hat fell on the dog's head,
Now he's prancing—where's my gin?

We drank the eggnog way too fast,
Now laughter echoes in our hearts.
Unruly friends are taking bets,
Whose turn is it to eat the tarts?

As garland drapes the awkward moments,
Joy becomes a game we play.
We'll dance until the lights go dim,
And make more memories today!

The Stillness Between the Lights

In the calm where shadows linger,
A holiday elf rings the bell.
But underneath the couch he hides,
Guess who won't be telling tales well?

Sparkle lights have turned to laughter,
Jumping jacks flew from the tree.
A squirrel's now using my living room,
Defining 'Christmas gaiety'!

We found the tinsel in the cat's claws,
Like frozen fish, it bounced and spun.
With every clumsy, friendly knock,
We end the night and call it fun.

The stillness talks in winking lights,
Whispers dance beneath the cheer.
This house of antics on a night,
Where joy and mischief reappear!

A Symphony of Sweet Nostalgia

Crinkled songs from ages past,
Play softly from the dusty mix.
A tune that makes the children laugh,
While grandma tries to shuffle tricks.

Ornaments are slung like wisdom,
A legend made of candy canes.
Each bite brings back a memory,
Not one that ever truly wanes.

We twirl around with messy flair,
Pine needles scatter like old tales.
With giggles rolling like the snow,
The night of fun never fails.

In the backdrop of jolly chaos,
Old tunes mash with new delight.
In every note, sweet laughter sings,
It's a symphony of pure night!

Scented Stories of the Ever-Bearing

The smell of pine and cookies blend,
Each whiff a chance for mischief more.
With flour dusting like powdered snow,
We race to see who's cooking score.

With every bauble, a great story,
Of fails and wins from years gone by.
A crooked angle here or there,
Reminds us laughter never dies.

Grandpa's tales grow wilder still,
As we munch on that sweet dessert.
He claims the dog has learned to dance,
While dancing, all of us get hurt!

So gather 'round the evergreen,
Beneath the glow of lights galore.
In scented stories that we spin,
Lies joy we constantly adore!

A Silence Adorned with Lights

In a corner shines a sight,
Sparkly balls and tinsel bright.
An elf caught snoozing on a limb,
Belly full from holiday whim.

The cat takes a daring leap,
Pawing at the ornaments deep.
Down they go in a clunk and crash,
Leaving behind a colorful splash.

Twinkling lights begin to sway,
A dance of chaos, come what may.
Grandma laughs, with a wink so sly,
While the cat just watches nearby.

Underneath, a puppy lays,
Dreaming of treats through the holiday haze.
A star on top begins to tilt,
Oh, the fun of unplanned spilt!

Tales Beneath the Boughs

Beneath the branches, secrets bloom,
A squirrel's quest, the living room.
With acorns tucked in every nook,
He thinks he's written quite the book.

A sock hung close, what's that surprise?
A slippery banana peel that lies!
The dog trots past, and oh so slick,
He takes a tumble, comically quick.

Flames dance in the fireplace glow,
While stockings bulge, all set for show.
'Tis the season for quite the cheer,
And laughs that echo year to year.

The star must have a mind of its own,
As it wiggles quietly, not alone.
A tale of fun, we won't forget,
Under green boughs, joy's silhouette.

The Frosted Heart's Recollection

On frosty nights, the memories twirl,
Like snowflakes caught in a joyful whirl.
With cocoa sipped in laughter fair,
And marshmallows tossed for the winter air.

A gingerbread man's been running free,
Hiding from all, but thirsty for tea.
He jumps with glee as kids rush in,
To munch him down with a giggly grin.

The garland swings with tales unspun,
Each ornament telling of festive fun.
A candy cane fight breaks out in glee,
As laughter fills the crisp, cold spree.

With every blink, more joy we find,
It's a frosted heart that leaves us kind.
In every corner, silly sights,
Recollections dance as holiday lights.

Echoes of Joy Amidst the Needles

Among the needles, echoes play,
With giggles shared throughout the day.
A pickle ornament, it's quite absurd,
Gives hints to games, not a word heard.

Mice in sweaters, ready for fun,
Scuttle around, chasing each one.
A ceiling fan spins, why not in glee?
It sends the tinsel dancing quite free.

Grandpa's hat, flopped on his head,
Gives him quite the look instead.
With baking woes and laughter's sound,
Amidst the needles, joy is found.

The night grows bright with plans anew,
Laughter rings as we create the brew.
Echoes of joy, they fit just right,
Beneath the glow of festive light.

Secrets Wrapped in Ribbons

Beneath the branches, secrets hide,
A cat with ornaments, full of pride.
He swats at lights that blink and glow,
While the cookies vanish, who can know?

A gift wrapped funny, it's lumpy and round,
Uncle Joe's sweater, it's quite profound!
A bow on top, askew and bizarre,
Chuckles arise - what a curious jar!

In tinsel and chaos, laughter flows,
Each mishap adds to our joyful shows.
With giggles wrapped tight in every cheer,
This season's antics really bring good cheer!

So raise your glass to the tree so tall,
With tangled lights, it's a glorious ball!
In stories of laughter, we find our way,
Happy moments, here in joyful play.

Chronicles of Natural Elegance

In green attire, with bulbs aglow,
Gifts stacked high - oh, what a show!
The dog steals pies with a cheeky grin,
As kids plot pranks to see who will win.

A squirrel drops twigs, oh what a mess!
Decorations hang in true distress.
While Auntie's fruitcake becomes a joke,
We laugh and munch on chocolate folk!

With glittery tales of mishaps bright,
A turkey chase under starry night.
Each laugh a branch, each sigh a string,
In these chronicles, joy takes wing!

Oh, toast to the chaos, the fun and glee,
For in the pandemonium, we all agree!
Life's little hiccups just make us dance,
In the magic of mistakes, we find romance.

A Treetop View of Hope

From up high, ornaments sway and tease,
As little hands reach for candy with ease.
The star's all askew, like a tiny hat,
There's laughter and giggles - imagine that!

A Christmas squirrel, cheeky and spry,
Steals a cookie and zips on by.
We stare in awe, mouths wide with glee,
Nature's own humor is plain to see!

In this froaden cheer, we find our grace,
A riddle of joy, from each furry face.
So gather around, let the stories round,
In mishaps and laughter, pure joy is found!

Raise up a cheer for the tale that stirs,
Each twinkling light, as laughter purrs!
In the heart of the season, hope spreads wide,
Through funny moments, let joy be our guide.

Embracing the Frost

With frost on the needles, a spark, a glow,
The neighbors have pies, but what do we know?
A snowman's carrot is slightly askew,
He dances around when the kids come to view.

A sleigh ride gone wrong, oh what a sight!
Dad falls in snow, what a comical fright!
As jingle bells jingle, it all turns to cheer,
In the chill of the season, we have no fear.

Laughter springs forth as we sing 'round the fire,
With marshmallows toasted, our hearts lift higher.
Embracing each giggle, each slip and each slide,
Together we find joy that cannot hide!

So let's raise our mugs, let the laughter uncoil,
In frosty embrace, through the snow and the toil.
For this is the season of silly delight,
In every small laugh, we find pure ignite!

Fragrant Memories in the Frost

Under twinkling lights so bright,
A squirrel took a leap in flight,
He mistook the star for a nut,
Now he's stuck in the branches' rut.

Ornaments hanging with such flair,
One slipped off and flew through the air,
It landed right on Grandpa's head,
Now he wears it like a crown in red.

The garland is tangled, oh what a sight,
Uncle Joe is wrestling it with delight,
He says it's a new dance he will show,
We're all laughing, oh how we glow!

Every year it's a glorious spree,
With laughter and chaos surrounding me,
Memory's fragrance, sweet and bright,
This frosty time, it's pure delight.

Magic Wrapped in Greenery

In a house decked out with strange decor,
A cat thinks it's a jungle to explore,
He pounces and tumbles, what a great show,
Leaving ribbons tangled in quite the row!

The lights flicker like a disco ball,
While Grandma's cookies tempt us all,
One bite in, they vanish so fast,
Sugar rush hits, we're dancing at last!

Underneath the boughs, stashed with glee,
A present for a clever little bee,
But it's wrapped too tight, it buzzed in fright,
Now it flits around in a flurry of light!

Oh, the stories this greenery holds,
With laughter and joy more precious than gold,
In every moment, there's magic so fine,
Wrapped in love like our favorite wine.

A Tapestry of Frosted Dreams

Each ornament spun with laughter's thread,
A mismatched sock on the tree instead,
It dangles so proudly, what a delight,
A fashion statement in the frosty night!

Each ribbon a tale, each bow a jest,
As Grandma insists her cookies are best,
But her secret? A pinch of salt instead,
Now we giggle at the crumbs she shed!

A snowman fashion show on the lawn,
Bobby's carrot nose has long since gone,
He wore mom's scarf, looking so dapper,
With birds chirping, what a grand clapper!

In the frost, we weave our cheer,
Creating memories year after year,
With laughter and love, the best of schemes,
In this tapestry of frosted dreams.

The Serenade of Winter's Bounty

Amidst the bows and glittering sights,
A bumblebee in winter fights,
It thought it was summer, oh what a blunder,
Now it buzzes, making kids wonder!

With sparkly hats and coats of fluff,
The kids say, 'is this enough?'
Mom rolls her eyes at the mess they make,
But laughter erupts, no hearts to break!

Each cookie baked with a sprinkle of cheer,
But oh, those sprinkles scattered near,
They found their way to the dog's long nose,
Now he's prancing, as if he knows!

Winter's bounty, a laughter's tune,
Dancing together under the moon,
With each silly moment, joy takes flight,
In this serenade of frosty night.

The Unseen Tales of Evergreens

In the corner, it stands so bright,
A sponge for all that twinkling light.
Underneath, old gifts still lie,
Wondering who forgot, oh my!

Bobbing baubles dangle tight,
Always waiting for that festive fight.
With cats and kids all in a scam,
Noble firs know the scheme—oh, scam!

Tinsel whispering secret things,
About the jingle bells and kinks,
Year by year, the tales unfold,
And of the popcorn garlands—bold.

Every ornament has a role,
From bright-eyed elf to doughnut stole.
With laughter echoing all around,
Evergreen tales in smiles abound.

Frost-Kissed Secrets of the Night

Underneath the starlit sky,
Ornaments flip, helping dreams fly.
With a wink, the icicles laugh,
But only at the fluffiest calf.

Snowflakes dance with little glee,
Chasing shadows, oh so free.
As the moon peers in surprise,
The tree just shrugs, it's all disguise.

Garlands knit old yarns untold,
While squirrels plot to raid the gold.
But nanas knew, in cozy cheer,
That gingerbread men might appear.

So toast to frost and all its fun,
As we wait, the night yet young.
With giggles echoing, snugly bright,
The secrets wait till morning light.

The Silent Sentinel of the Season

Standing tall in living rooms,
Ever patient while chaos blooms.
A tower of twinkling lights,
Hiding tales of festive flights.

Cats cozy up, while kids all race,
To take those charms and find their space.
Chasing bubbles, giggling loud,
While pine needles lay proud, but bowed.

Tinsel tangles, oh what a plight,
As the lights flicker with pure delight.
The wise old tree just shakes its head,
Knowing well what lies ahead.

In the corner, secrets spill,
Of feasts to come and jolly thrill.
A nod to the past and laughs to share,
Evergreens hold more love than air.

A Whisper in Woodland Silence

Pine perfume drifts through the air,
As elves sneak snacks without a care.
Underneath the branches low,
Squirrels scurry for their show.

Lights that twinkle, stories tease,
While gnomes swap tales with the breeze.
Christmas wishes floating near,
Tickling frost upon the sphere.

Garland strands whisperer secrets,
While crafty hands misplace the beets.
Snowmen snicker in the yard,
Sharing rumblings, life's not hard.

So gather 'round, oh merry crew,
The woodland's hush holds laughter, too.
A wink, a nod to all that's bright,
The whispers sing of pure delight.

Light in the Shadows of Winter

In a corner stood a spruce, so green,
With tinsel dreams, a sparkle unseen.
The cats in the garland, oh what a sight,
They plot and they plan, in the quiet of night.

A star on the top, so proudly it beams,
While reindeer dance, lost in their schemes.
The lights twinkle on, a flicker and flash,
As the dog chases shadows, with a comical crash.

Mismatched bulbs, a Christmas delight,
One's blinking fast, the other's too bright.
The family laughs, in a hug and a cheer,
For the quirkiest moments that bring them near.

So raise up your glasses, let merriment flow,
For the tree tells a tale, in its own wobbly show!
With laughter and joy, we gather around,
In the spirit of winter, our love knows no bounds.

Memories in a Winter Glow

Once every year, we gather anew,
With scarves and with hats, and old slippers too.
The lights strung with care, but one's out again,
Lighting up memories, in laughter refrain.

Cookies and milk left for a jolly old man,
While the dog sniffs the gifts, as only he can.
The kids set the stage with their giggles and glee,
As the tree shakes with joy, or maybe just me.

Fuzzy socks worn, a fashion misfire,
Grandma's sweater burns with a fruity desire.
With stories we share, and a toast from the cat,
May your winter be blessed, with as much love as that!

So gather round closely, with cheer in the air,
For the best part of Christmas is simply to care.
With lights, laughter, and joy as our guide,
In this chaotic winter, let happiness glide.

The Pine's Hidden Memories

In the living room sits a noble old pine,
With needles like memories, green and divine.
The ornaments tell tales from years long ago,
Of mishaps and laughter, and most of all – snow.

Here comes Uncle Bob with a homemade delight,
His fruitcake is legendary, a fearsome sight.
As we taste and we laugh, we all know the truth,
That dessert is a monster, of eternal youth.

The lights flicker low, a battle with fate,
One bulb, in defiance, decides to be late.
But the laughter surrounds like a warm, fuzzy quilt,
In this season of love, our joy never wilt.

So cheer to the chaos, the giggles, the mess,
For each quirk in our family is such a sweet bless.
With stories and giggles, we make quite a scene,
In the heart of the holidays, we're all evergreen.

Roots of a Timeless Tradition

In the corner it stands, our holiday cheer,
Each branch a story, some far, some near.
The kids try to hide gifts, but mischief they weave,
As Dad finds his socks tucked under the leaves.

Grandma's old angel, her crown slightly askew,
Sits on top proudly, with a wink just for you.
The dog snags the garland, a master of stealth,
In his quest for more treats, he's a thief of good health!

The snowflakes outside dance with icy grace,
While we sit, all together, a smile on each face.
With cocoa in hand, we toast to the light,
May the spirit of laughter fill every night.

So gather your loved ones, both near and afar,
In the roots of tradition, you'll find who you are.
With joy and with jokes, let the memories unfold,
For this whimsical winter, is a treasure to hold.

Timeless Treasures in the Dark

In a corner stands a grand old sprout,
Its ornaments dance, give a clout.
A tinsel draped like grandma's hair,
Whispers secrets from a time so rare.

Lights flicker like they're in a race,
Some bulbs are lost, in a tangled space.
Elves start to giggle, their jokes on cue,
While cookies seem to vanish, who knew?

A spell of laughter fills the room,
As cats chase jingle bells with a zoom.
Pine needles fall like confetti rain,
Each drop a giggle, soft but plain.

With gifts stacked high, a pyramid swell,
One's a sock, oh what the hell?
The ornaments wink, they're in the know,
Next year, they plan a wild show!

Silent Vigil of the Night

The tree stands guard through frosty air,
Its branches weave a tale to share.
A star atop, it holds its breath,
Giggles hidden, awaiting the heist.

The elves conspire on who gets to peek,
A fragile bulb shakes, a little squeak.
Beneath the bows, a lurking cat,
Prowling softly, imagine that!

A ribbon rolls like a runaway car,
Hearts burst with laughter from near and far.
What's this? A present with no tag?
Socks for the dog? Oh, what a brag!

With cookie crumbs in tracks so bold,
The story of winter, sweetly told.
Lights dimmed low, the night feels right,
Silly secrets spill with delight!

A Glow of Nostalgia

A glow in the dark, where memories gleam,
Each ornament hums a forgotten theme.
Grandpa's old hat, on a branch with flair,
Spinning tales of yesterdays rare.

Mittens from childhood, a comical sight,
Red, green, and fuzzy, oh what a fright!
Ribbons untangled in a clumsy dance,
I wonder if they recall their chance?

Whispers of laughter, a scent of pie,
Jolly old tunes make us sigh.
Wrapped-up thoughts, what will they decree?
That time's sweeter, like honeyed tea!

Beneath the glow, the world falls asleep,
While pride and joy, the memories keep.
The tree bursts with stories big and small,
Reminding us all, we've had a ball!

Musings in the Midnight Snow

Midnight strikes, a blanket of white,
Under the tree, we share delight.
Snowflakes dance, they swirl and twirl,
While dreams of Christmas begin to unfurl.

Pine-scented laughter fills the frost,
Each giggle a treasure, nothing is lost.
Socks still missing, who would have guessed?
The mischievous elf is surely blessed!

Gifts wrapped oddly, a box with a shoe,
Must be a prank, oh what a view!
Cider's sweet warmth and cookies galore,
A feast for all, who could ask for more?

As bells jingle softly on this starry night,
The world's hush feels perfectly right.
A silent story, tucked away tight,
Growing with giggles till morning's bright!

A Tangle of Traditions

Once a needle fell, and behold,
It danced on the floor, all brave and bold.
A cat leapt high, oh what a sight,
Chasing the chaos through the night.

Uncle Joe brought lights that blink and hum,
While Auntie Betty's cookie dough does glum.
Together they bicker, yet burst into cheer,
For laughter's the gift that brings us near.

The star on top keeps tilting down,
As Grandpa mumbles, making us frown.
But we all can't help but love the blur,
Of tangled lights that start to stir.

Through ribbons and papers, the mess is grand,
Yet hearts unite, we hold hands.
In this tangle of joy so bright and wild,
It's just like family, oh so mild!

The Glow of Silent Blessings

Under a glow that flickers and shakes,
We try to sing carols, but all it breaks.
A dog in a sweater snorts with delight,
As we snicker at his rather poor plight.

Mismatched socks become the newest trend,
As Dad laughs with glee, his spirit to mend.
Through quiet giggles and whispers so low,
Cheers rise like snowflakes, all set to blow.

Pine-scented wishes fill the cool air,
While Cousin Tim rants about life and hair.
The blender hums joy for our festive drinks,
And how it all tumbles, oh, how it blinks!

We cozy up close, heartbeats in tune,
Like a balloon that floats near the moon.
In moments we find beneath the lights' show,
Are silent blessings wrapped soft in glow.

Memory's Lanterns in the Dark

Flickering memories fill the night sky,
As Grandpa recalls how he once learned to fly.
With tales of mishaps and giggles galore,
We roll on the floor, begging for more.

A spoonful of fruitcake, oh what a fate,
That Aunt Suzy just baked, we're all set to rate.
But the laughter blooms louder than cake on the plate,
As we giggle and moan, it's quite the debate.

The ornaments dangle like quirks on a tree,
With stories behind them, they wriggle with glee.
With memories woven like garland so bright,
They shine in the chaos that twirls in the night.

So gather around with lanterns so warm,
In tales that we spin, together the norm.
In the merry moments that twinkle in dark,
We weave our own story, a hilarious spark!

Ornamented Echoes of the Past

Ornaments nestled in dusty old boxes,
Transport us back to those rather fine faxes.
With a snowman that wobbles, quite proud on the shelf,
Each echo of laughter, a memory of self.

Tinsel's a headache, one big shiny mess,
As little ones giggle, their pure joy to stress.
They hang candy canes, but oh what a mess!
They start to devour, their sweet tooth's finesse.

Old poems recited in voices so bright,
Bring giggles and chuckles, oh what a delight!
As Grandma plays games with a wink and a twirl,
Like a Christmas party held in a whirl.

Though echoes of past might just fade away,
The laughter remains, so we're here to stay.
In ornaments' shimmer, we dance to the tune,
Of merry old memories beneath the moon.

Bowls of Light and Dreams

In the living room, it stands so tall,
Covered in tinsel, it seems to call.
The cat thinks it's her new favorite toy,
Pouncing and prancing, oh what a joy!

Decorations hang, but one's gone astray,
A cheeky elf took it for a play.
Dad laughs so hard, nearly spills his drink,
While Mom just sighs and starts to think.

The smell of pine, oh, what a treat,
With glittering balls and desserts to eat.
Grandma sneaks cookies, crumbs on her chin,
The pets join in, ready to win!

But as the night falls and laughter swells,
We share our secrets, and everyone tells.
It's the stories we share that bring out the cheer,
As bowls of light shine bright this year.

Stars Caught in the Canopy

Up in the branches, a star takes a dive,
It lands on the dog; we see him thrive!
He prances around, a bright little sight,
Chasing his tail beneath moon's light.

Mom thinks it's elegance, with fine flair,
Till Uncle Joe trips; it's chaos in there.
A *CRASH!* and a clatter, an ornament falls,
Now it's a game of dodge the Christmas balls!

With giggles and grins, the night carries on,
As we tell tales till the break of dawn.
Stars stuck in foliage shower us bright,
In this merry gathering, all feels just right.

Wrapped in our joy, we dance and we sing,
As night twinkles softly, a magical thing.
Laughter and twinkling lights twine and swirl,
This is the magic in our festive world.

Hidden Wishes Amongst the Foliage

In the dark of night, whispers arise,
From leaves and lights, like sweet little sighs.
A wish was made on a brittle twig,
By someone who dreamt of a dance so big!

The garland giggles, what a sight to see,
As it tickles the dog, oh so carefree!
Mom's hidden snickers, Dad's stifled glee,
With every small twist, more fun there will be.

Children tiptoe, all wrapped in their dreams,
Searching for magic under twinkling beams.
Whispers of wishes float high in the air,
The secrets of Christmas, a bond we all share.

So gather 'round, with cocoa in hand,
As we tell our stories, oh, isn't it grand?
Hidden wishes in foliage swirl,
Like giggles and laughter, they twirl and unfurl.

The Garland's Whispered Legacy

A garland sits tired, woven with care,
It seems to listen, in its green wear.
While we hang it low, it wiggles its leaves,
Chuckling at all of our festive reprieves.

A memory escapes from the string of lights,
Of a hamster who gleefully climbed the heights.
With Grandma's reminder and giggly delight,
"Remember the chaos? That was quite the night!"

Tinsel confetti rains down with a plop,
As Dad tries to clean up, but whoops—he can't stop!
"Next year," he grins, "we'll put it in bags!"
But laughter erupts; we all wave our flags.

Each twist of the garland remembers well,
All those great stories we're eager to tell.
So here's to the laughter, the mess, and the cheer,
In the whispers of garlands, our love shines clear!

Whispers of Evergreen

In the corner, standing tall,
With ornaments that love to brawl.
The lights blink in a crazy dance,
While cats plot a daring prance.

Needles drop like secrets told,
As kids spot magic, bright and bold.
A squirrel sneaks in for a feast,
While we all pretend to be least.

The star atop winks with delight,
As tangled ribbons start to fight.
Mom laughs as she finds a shoe,
Right next to that old rubber goose.

Beneath its boughs, we gather tight,
Sharing jokes, all pure delight.
This tree's got stories wrapped in cheer,
Who knew such fun could come from here?

Tinsel's Tale

Once a strand all shiny and bright,
Now a cat's new favorite bite.
Twinkling tales from days of yore,
Fluffy friends explored before.

The lights flicker, like winking eyes,
Squirrels giggle, oh what a surprise!
Dad's stuck in lights, what a sight,
While Mom just laughs, 'You'll be alright!'

Garland flutters, like it has sass,
Who knew it could dance with such class?
Each bow tied with the utmost care,
Yet somehow, it's all in the air.

At the end of the evening's fun,
We find gifts for everyone.
But wait—what's that? A present for me?
Is it tinsel? Oh, let it be!

Underneath the Boughs

A cozy spot where shadows play,
Kids peek out, shouting 'Hooray!'
Underneath the branches wide,
Giggles loud, you can't hide.

Beneath the lights so bright and bold,
We tell each other tales retold.
An elf stumbles with sticky tape,
Oh no! Now he is in a scrape!

Pinecones rolling, what a mess,
Dogs dive in with pure finesse.
Socks are puppets joined by fate,
It's all a jolly, silly state.

Cookies vanish at record speed,
As laughter bursts, it's all we need.
Under these arms, joy wraps tight,
What a magical, merry night!

Sparkling Secrets of the Night

Glimmers gather, smiles abound,
With mischief lurking all around.
A sneaky mouse steals a treat,
While we dance to a funny beat.

The star's gone bonkers, prefers to wobble,
As prankster gifts create a bobble.
A twist, a turn—oh dear, what's this?
Our secret snack has gone amiss!

Decorations hang with flair,
While laughter fills the evening air.
Tangled lights are quite the scene,
Who knew fun could be so keen?

And as the night draws all to close,
We find peace, in laughter it shows.
These moments wrapped in joy will stay,
The night shines bright, in its own way!

Milton Keynes UK
Ingram Content Group UK Ltd.
UKHW022011131124
451149UK00013B/1111